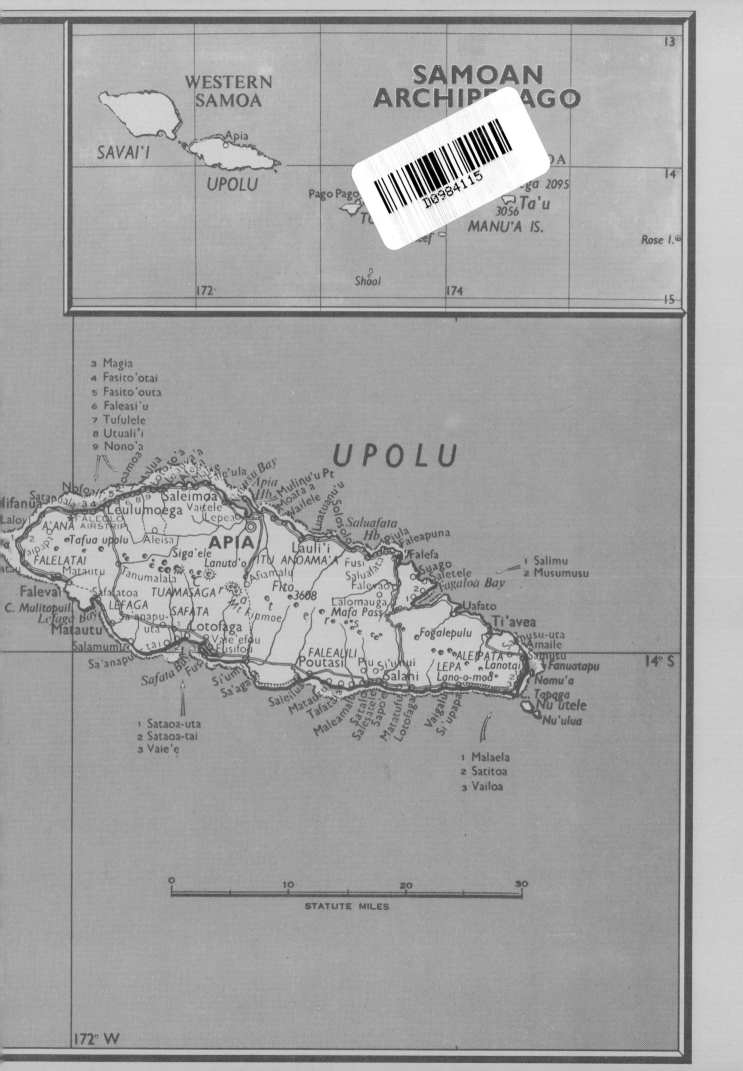

SAMOAN ARCHIPELAGO

WESTERN SAMOA

SAVAI'I

Apia

UPOLU

Pago Pago

...ga 2095

Ta'u

3056

MANU'A IS.

Rose I.

Shoal

13

14

15

172

174

UPOLU

3 Magia
4 Fasito'otai
5 Fasito'outa
6 Faleasi'u
7 Tufulele
8 Utuali'i
9 Nono'a

...oamoa

Lotoio'a

...le'ula Bay

Apia

Mulinu'u Pt

Nofoa

Satapu...

3 4 5

6 8 9

Saleimoa

Vaitele

Moata'a

Wailele

...fanua

Leulumoega

Lepea

Luatuanu'u

Solosolo

Saluafata

Laloy'i

FALEOLO

A'ANA AIRSTRIP

Hb. piula

Faleapuna

Tafua upolu

Aleisa

APIA

Lauli'i

Saluafata

Falefa

FALELATAI

Siga'ele

Lanuto'o

ITU ANOAMA'A

Fusi

Suago

Saletele

1 Salimu

2 Musumusu

Matautu

Tanumalala

Afiamalu

Faleao

Fito

3608

Mt Fito

Lalomauga

Fagaloa Bay

Falevai

Safatoa

TUAMASAGA

Mafa Pass

Uafato

C. Mulitapuili

LEFAGA

Sa'anapu-uta

SAFATA

Ti'avea

Lefaga Bay

Lotofaga

Vaie'efou

Fogalepulu

...usu-uta

Amaile

Matautu

Vaie'efou

FALEALILI

Poutasi

Piu Si'umui

ALEIPATA

Samusu

Salamumu

Sa'anapu-tai

2 3

Fusifou

Salani

LEPA

Lanotai

Fanuatapu

Safata Bay

Fusi

Si'umu

Sa'aga

Saleilua

Lano-o-moa

Namu'a

1 Sataoa-uta

2 Sataoa-tai

3 Vaie'e

Matautu

Tafatafa

Saleaumua

Matatufu

Lotofaga

Vaigalu

Si'upapa

Tapaga

Nu'utele

Nu'ulua

1 Malaela

2 Satitoa

3 Vailoa

14° S

172° W

0 ____ 10 ____ 20 ____ 30

STATUTE MILES

SAMOA IN COLOUR

samoa in colour

JAMES SIERS

A.H. & A.W. REED Wellington/Sydney/London

First published 1970
Reprinted 1974

A.H. & A.W. REED LTD
182 Wakefield Street, Wellington
29 Dacre Street, Artarmon, NSW 2064
11 Southampton Row, London WC1B 5HA
also
29 Dacre Street, Auckland
165 Cashel Street, Christchurch

ISBN 0 589 00455 7

Printed and bound by
Kyodo Prining Co. Ltd.,
Tokyo, Japan.

CONTENTS

INTRODUCTION

DUE TO AN ACCIDENT of history there is only one Samoa but two Samoan political states, the Independent State of Western Samoa and the United States Territory of Eastern Samoa.

Like all the other territories in the Pacific, Samoa became engulfed in the final wave of colonial expansion towards the end of the nineteenth century, when the European powers and the United States bartered among themselves for the last few showpieces of colonial wealth and power.

Samoa was formerly annexed by two colonial powers in 1900—relatively late in comparison with other Pacific territories. The United States took Tutuila and the islands of Manu'a, while Germany annexed the rich islands of Savai'i, Upolu and other outlying islands.

German Samoa was taken over by New Zealand at the outbreak of the First World War, and was administered by New Zealand as a Trust Territory until 1962, when it became independent. Eastern Samoa is still American, and given the choice, the people would no doubt vote to remain under Washington's aegis. The Federal Government looks after them benevolently with a yearly budget of eight to nine million dollars, which coupled with the five million dollars generated locally, gives the 27,000 people in this State little to grumble about. Western Samoa has none of this affluence, but it does possess something more rare—a unique way of life and a pride in its status as the only independent Polynesian nation.

The two States lie divided by approximately eighty miles of water. If you look at a map of the region you will see that the chain of islands lies in a west to south-east direction. At the westernmost point is Savai'i, the biggest island of the group. It is a beautiful island, with a changing landscape of high mountains, the highest rising to over 6,000 feet. It has broad lagoons, flows of volcanic lava, and the most beautiful villages in the world. In economic terms it is an undeveloped island, but attractive because of this. A rough road skirts it, but apart from infrequent buses there is almost no traffic and life goes on much as it did centuries ago.

Slightly to the south-east, separated by a stretch of water some fifteen miles wide, is Upolu. In the strait between the two are the islands of Apolima and Manono, both inhabited.

Slightly smaller than Savai'i, Upolu is the administrative centre of this tiny independent nation, and as such boasts many more amenities. It has an airport, better roads, including a new one from the airport to Apia, and the city of Apia itself with a modern port.

At the eastern tip of Upolu there is a number of small inhabited islands and from this point it is about twenty minutes by air to Tutuila, the administrative centre of American Samoa. Tutuila is perhaps the most spectacular island of the Samoan Archipelago. Tortured and twisted in shape, it is a giant lava-rock outcrop, chiseled down from its highest points into a series of deep valleys, fiord-like bays and sheer cliff faces, all covered with palms, native trees, and shrubs sheltering taro patches among the silvery waterfalls. A narrow reef surrounds the island, but in some places such as Tafuna or Steps Point, the giant seas, driven by the trades, crash straight into the lava shooting waterspouts higher than the coconut trees.

Eighty miles east again are the islands of Manu'a, whose ferocious warriors were once the scourge of their much bigger neighbours.

It is hard to believe that Western and American Samoa can be so entirely different. Western Samoa still depends predominantly on a subsistence economy, whereas their neighbours are more cash economy oriented. Western Samoa is preoccupied with its intricate political system, while American Samoa looks towards Washington. Western Samoans speak English with a unique accent; American Samoans speak English with an American accent (and Western Samoans observe wryly that they also speak Samoan with an American accent). It is strange to hear a waitress or an official answer in English "You're welcome, sir," after you have thanked them in Samoan.

There are other incongruous differences between the two Samoas. At a social ceremony in Western Samoa the villagers strike you as Samoan; in American Samoa their more opulent "native" dress, plus the inevitable dark glasses and cigars, give you the feeling that here indeed, you're on to something unusual. These differences will multiply as time goes by, unless the two States unite. This is unlikely in the forseeable future, despite the attitude of High Chief Fuimaono of American Samoa, who would like to see such a union.

To understand how this extraordinary state of affairs came about it is necessary to look at the history of Samoa.

Archaeologists and ethnologists now believe that this group of islands was a key to the eventual Polynesian settlement of Eastern Polynesia, including Hawaii to the north and New Zealand to the extreme south. Earlier authorities, such as Sir Peter Buck, felt that the Polynesian migration had moved through Micronesia, to reach the Marquesas and Tahiti, from where it dispersed again. Now, it is believed that the Polynesians came through Indonesia and the Philippines to the Solomons, the New Hebrides, and Fiji before they sailed towards Tonga and Samoa.

Those early migrants were a hardy, sea-faring, warlike people, already subscribing to an intricate social system which, along with coconuts, pigs, chickens, taro, breadfruit, kumara and yams, they brought to make life better in their new lands.

This is what authorities, apart from such iconoclasts as Thor Heyerdahl, believe. What the Samoans believe is quite different. They believe they came from nowhere; they were there from the beginning of the world. And it pays not to argue, for the Samoan has been known to say that where else, if not in Samoa, could God have made the original Garden of Eden?

However they got there the Samoan story, like the rest of the settlement of the Pacific, is one of the wonders of this world. Their canoes were large sailing craft with twin hulls of seventy feet or more lashed together with durable sennit, giving the craft the stability of the modern catamaran, which has borrowed the principle from Polynesian navigators. On the platform between the two hulls stood the shelter. Provisions, each stored according to the order of its importance, crowded the hulls and deck space. A fireplace, carefully constructed on the planking, glowed on a carpet of sand. Pigs, dogs and chickens, confined to their appointed places, took their chances on the skill of the captain and the luck of the course he had chosen.

It is now fashionable to say that the Polynesians had no navigating skill, and that the vast area of the Pacific was settled through accidental drifts, but there is much evidence to the contrary. They knew navigation and used it on extensive voyages throughout the Pacific during various phases of their history.

There are too many legends in each of the island groups which refer to long voyages, both for conquest and exploration, for us to believe that these are merely part of an elaborate myth. There was also a wealth of specific reference during the early years of European contact to long beyond-the-horizon voyages. Tupaia, former high priest of Taputapuatea, at Opoa on the island of Raiatea, escaped from that island and sailed to Tahiti when his home was invaded and taken by the people of Bora Bora. He sailed with Captain Cook, and knew the position of various islands and their approximate distances, named the ones he had visited and then, as the ship touched Java in Indonesia, laid down a course which he said would take the ship back to Tahiti.

Tupaia died before it could be put to the test, but other navigators met voyaging canoes in mid-ocean and can testify to the confidence of the people in these ships. One such Tongan canoe was seen in mid-ocean by HMS *Pandora*, the naval ship sent to ferret out the mutineers of the *Bounty*. This canoe, under the famous Tongan navigator Kau Moala, had been on a great voyage, calling at Samoa and Fiji, among other islands, before going home. The navigator knew perfectly well where he had been and how to get home from there, although the distance covered in total would have been close to 2,000 miles.

In parts of the Pacific the ancient methods are still used. Take Micronesia. Possibly even now traditional forms of navigation are still taught—they certainly were two years ago when a young American anthropologist I met was there. The people think nothing of sailing 800 miles across the open ocean, and until quite recently it was obligatory for each island to send representatives to an annual gathering.

This navigation school taught the use of the sun and stars, seasonal winds, the determination of currents and of the effect of the various waves upon the course set. It was essential to be a good judge of the weather and seldom were voyages made in the wrong season.

Navigators who discovered new islands recorded the course with poetry or song which laid down explicitly how to reach them. Thus the great fleet which left Rarotonga for New Zealand in 1350 AD could sail confidently, as did many of the captains, who took their craft the long distance from Tahiti to Hawaii in the North.

Though navigating ability was of paramount importance and navigators in Polynesian communities were admired much as our most eminent scientists are today, it was the construction of the canoes and their seaworthiness which were the greatest tributes to the skill of the peoples of Polynesia and the Pacific in general. Canoes were constructed out of a log, adzed into a hull, the hull built up by planking, itself adzed to fit perfectly, before being caulked and sealed with breadfruit paste and coconut husk.

The little *paopao* you see in the lagoons of Samoa, however well constructed, can give you little idea of the beauty of the large outrigger craft or the big double canoes. Inevitably, the most ambitious chiefs had the best double canoes and paid a great deal to get them. The craftsmen who built them believed that their power came direct from the gods of the sea and approached their task as a divine directive. They knew full well the weakness of any fault, particularly in the lashing of the various parts together. In Tahiti, the craftsmen would sing:

What have I, O Tane,
Tane, god of beauty!
'Tis sennit,
'Tis sennit from the host of heaven,
'Tis sennit of thine, O Tane!
Thread it from the inside, it comes outside.
Thread it from the outside, it goes inside.
Tie it firmly, bind it fast.
This sennit of thine, O Tane,
Make it hold, make it hold.
It cannot weaken,
It cannot loosen,
When bound with sacred sennit,
With thy sacred sennit, O Tane.

Thus firmly bound, caulked, stocked with provisions for the voyagers, they hoisted their sails of pandanus matting and faced the open sea. Great steering oars, handled by two or three men, kept the craft on course. In a good wind the craft fairly skimmed along, giving the canoes better times than the sailing ships of the first Europeans to venture into the Pacific.

The Polynesians also had what few others possessed—the ability to survive should they, by storm or misadventure, miss their objective. Some of the most remarkable stories ever told, such as that of Minerva Reef—when a party of Tongans went off course and survived for 100 days sheltering in an old Japanese hulk on a reef which was exposed only at low tide—or that of the drift of several Cook Islanders from Rakahanga to the Hebrides, a distance of over 2000 miles, concern extraordinary ability. Given the barest essentials, they will live. The Tongans who were wrecked on Minerva Reef survived as much on their heritage as they did on the meagre rations they could get at low tide.

Those Polynesian sailors who first saw the green, cloud-topped mountains of their Samoa must have marvelled at the sight. Once having landed they would have thanked their gods for having guided them to this warm, rich, fertile soil.

What needed to be done the new settlers would quickly effect. Plants would be sown; houses built; the bush explored, and possibly a canoe sent back to tell others of the new discovery.

It is probably fair to assume that the initial period of settlement and colonisation was the most peaceful in the history of Samoa. But once the population had built up, the stage was set for war, for the Polynesians were a warlike race.

The Samoan social system was based on the extended family unit whose interests were administered by the appointed leader, the *matai*. In the intricate way that life developed, some families through their war abilities assumed greater power in their villages, and extended this to larger districts and during odd periods of Samoan history, to hold sway over the entire group. To safeguard this power, the leaders of these families were granted titles which their descendants bear to this day.

Life in the Samoan village, even now, follows an age-old pattern established and embellished by these early colonists. The village consists of a neat arrangement of *fales*, usually facing a common, their sides open to the cooling breeze. Behind them are the cooking huts, usually no more than a shelter against rain. These are often set on the very edge of plantations, which run back into the mountains. The family, with its clearly defined set of duties, works for a common cause. All they produce is theoretically the *matai's*. He, according to time-honoured custom, distributes it as he sees fit. Ideally, the system works well, but it does not take much perception to see that a bad *matai* can have an unhappy influence on his family.

The Samoans needed little excuse to start the wars which were fought between villages, and later between districts. Early visitors to Samoa said that war there was a way of life. If there were no cause they would make one. Possibly this was due to the easy life and to the background of the Samoans. The very characteristics which had made them succeed in their daring voyages were the ones which war heightened—courage, leadership, strength and cunning.

Perhaps it was due to the bitter feuds which had arisen between the leading families that first the Fijians and later the Tongans were able to assert themselves in Samoa. Little is known of the Fijian intrusion. It has been suggested that Fijian raiders established themselves in Manu'a from where they held the rest of Samoa to ransom.

The Tongan invasion is better authenticated. Probably by using the same tactics that Europeans were to adopt later the Tongans came as friendly voyagers with an eye on the main chance. They would soon tip the balance of power by aiding a chief willing to make common cause with them, beat his adversaries and then in turn hold their host in thrall. They were successful, and took over the entire island group for a period of over 100 years

10

until they were driven out by the Malietoa family, whose title descends from that last historic battle. The Tongans, beaten and pulling out in their canoes, heard their chief shout to the successful Samoans: "Malie tau, malie toa,"—"well fought, brave warrior". Thus today's Head of State of Western Samoa is named Malietoa.

The Samoans settled down once more to internal strife and warfare until the eighteenth century, when European exploration was reaching its height in the Pacific. The first navigator credited with the discovery of Samoa is the Dutchman Jacob Roggeveen, in 1722. He fixed the position of the group inaccurately and sailed away without landing. Next came the Frenchman, Bougainville, and shortly after him, La Perouse, who lost twelve men during a shore skirmish at Asu, on Tutuila Island.

Until 1830 the islands escaped official European interest. Beachcombers established themselves there, but as yet no naval ships interfered.

Looking at it from the safe distance of time it is easy to see how colonial exploitation developed. The Pacific was being partitioned between Britain, Germany, France, and the United States, and Samoa was a rich prize. The United States, though officially opposed to colonisation, was nevertheless looking for suitable harbours in the area. The greatest interest in Samoa was shown by Germany, Britain, and the United States, whose navies soon arrived to watch each other in the roadstead in Apia and whose officers aided the various Samoan factions seeking to control the islands.

As the Tongans had done earlier, European powers were to do now—divide and rule. But first there had to be an understanding between the three powers as to who would get ultimate control of Samoa.

In the meantime there was some attempt to maintain Samoa as an independent state, usually under the rule of a "king" temporarily accepted, willingly or otherwise, from the principal chiefly families who laid claim to the title. In the forty years before the islands were finally divided between Germany and the United States, half a dozen kings were crowned, some of them more than twice.

The wars in support of the rival factions reached a new intensity. Since the 1830s European beachcombers and traders had introduced alcohol and guns as principal trade goods. It was a volatile combination. Christianity, though readily accepted from the Rev. John Williams of the London Missionary Society, and later from the Wesleyans and Catholics, preached against violence, but the Samoans were quick to perceive the rivalry that the churches encouraged between their faiths. They were also quick to see that the naval ships which began to gather in Apia carried guns and marines, and that their captains, though holding divine service on Sundays, nevertheless were quick to order a bombardment should the necessity arise.

By the 1850s trading stations were well-established and various chiefs were heavily in debt to these companies because they felt it necessary to obtain muskets, powder, and ball at all costs. Land was mortgaged to such an extent that before 1900 Europeans laid claim to more land than the islands of Samoa possessed in total. Robert Louis Stevenson, who arrived in Samoa in 1890, evoked the mood of those early times in his story *The Beach at Falesa*.

The one factor which made Samoa more turbulent than other island groups was the entry of Germany as a contending power. German interests were developed with the arrival of August Unshelm in Apia in 1856. A man of great energy and ability, Unshelm developed a master colonisation plan for Germany in the Pacific. As a representative of the firm Johann Cesar Godeffroy und Sohn of Hamburg, he came ostensibly to trade, but he knew that his best trading advantages could only be developed if Samoa were annexed by Germany.

Godeffroy already had interests in the Pacific. There was a copra processing plant at

Cochin and trade representatives as far away as South America. Unshelm expanded to Fiji and Tonga. His untimely death in a hurricane in Fiji in 1861 did not check German expansion. His successor Theodor Weber possessed the same energy, drive and intelligence. He built on Unshelm's work and within five years had expanded German interests to a vast area of the Pacific. He opened trading stations at Niue, Futuna, the Gilbert and Ellice group, the Tokelaus, and Wallis; and to the west he reached the great islands of the Solomon chain, the Hebrides, New Britain, New Ireland and Nauru as well as the scattered atolls of the Marshall-Mariana and Caroline groups. Throughout most of these areas his firm also began a land acquisition programme, which in Samoa alone was responsible for 75,000 acres.

This rapid expansion had its obvious political implications. Britain, whose interests in the Pacific were established with the colonisation of Australia and New Zealand, sent naval ships to watch the Germans. The Americans sent warships to watch both the British and the Germans. Each faction had its consuls ashore, whose demands they tended to reinforce at the point of a gun. Thus, they acted on wrongs meted out by the Samoans to their nationals. When in 1856 an Englishman named Fox was murdered at Savai'i, the wrong was squared two years later by the captain of HMS *Cordelia*. He called at the village and burned houses and canoes till the murderer was surrendered. He then hanged him from the yardarm of his ship and left him dangling for all to see. Thereafter native behaviour, traders noted, improved considerably.

From 1860 to 1870 Godeffroy's interests went ahead at an accelerated pace. In 1870, however, they received a setback from which they never recovered. The Franco-Prussian war caused Hamburg to be blockaded and Godeffroy went bankrupt. With the firm's collapse, the colonisation plan was put aside. Godeffroy's was taken over by Deutsche Handles und Plantagen Gesellschaft der Sudsee Inseln zu Hamburg.

But rivalry between Germany, Britain and the United States remained, and unleashed on Samoa some of its most bitter wars.

American interest in Samoa had developed with the Wilkes expedition in 1839. Commander Charles Wilkes brought in six ships which had been specially outfitted for a scientific and hydrographic expedition of the Pacific. He mapped and measured while his scientists recorded the islands' flora and fauna. Wilkes met Malietoa Vainu'upo, a leading chief, and arranged a treaty with him and other chiefs, setting up regulations governing visiting ships. Among the Europeans who were beachcombing in Samoa from early days were several Americans, including a Captain James Stewart, who claimed some 300,000 acres. He was active in Tutuila and persuaded some chiefs to ask for United States annexation. But Washington refused, and Stewart faded into obscurity.

In 1871, when German, British and American rivalry was at its highest, W.H. Webb, of New York, began a shipping service to the Pacific, with calls at Samoa. In 1875 the Pacific Mail Steamship Company of San Francisco followed in his wake. Wilkes, supported by Webb, urged their Government to annex Tutuila, claiming that Pago harbour was "the finest in the Pacific". In 1872 Commander R.W. Meade of the United States Navy steamed into Pago aboard the *Narragansett*. His mission was to report on the possibility of establishing a naval station there.

Meade found British and American settlers in Samoa worried about the growing German influence. He saw the advantage of Pago harbour and promptly signed with chief Mauga a treaty which gave the United States exclusive rights to the harbour, in return for "friendship and protection". This treaty, though never ratified, accelerated the rivalry between the three powers so that the navies of Britain and Germany began to take a more active role.

The following year Colonel A.B. Steinberger of Maryland arrived in Samoa, styling himself as a "special agent" of the Department of State. He was appointed through his friendship with President Grant and appears to have come with a sincere desire to help the Samoan people. He told the Samoan people to stop making individual land grants to outsiders and interceded in peace negotiations between Malietoa Laupepa and Malietoa Talavou, two of the chief contenders to the title.

Malietoa Laupepa became king and Steinberger helped him draft a constitution. He canvassed the leading chiefs as well as Malietoa and then went back to Washington to persuade the Government to annex the islands. The Senate refused and Steinberger returned to Samoa as an "unsalaried" agent of the United States. The warship *Tuscarora* which brought him to Apia created a favourable impression and a letter from the commander said that Steinberger would help the Samoan people in organising their Government as an independent nation. Within a short time he became the power behind Laupepa's throne and when the country was threatened with yet another war through another claim to the throne of Tupua Pulepule, Steinberger organised alternative four-year terms for the two rivals.

Though he appeared to be sincere towards the Samoan people, Steinberger was in fact working for German interests. The American consul discovered Steinberger's duplicity and in collusion with the British had him deported to Fiji. Steinberger, however, had the last laugh. He brought action against the consul and had him relieved of his post, while the captain of the British ship which took him to Fiji was court martialled and reprimanded.

Steinberger's removal exposed the rivalries again and led to a new outbreak of fighting. A delegation of chiefs sought British annexation, but was refused. It went to Washington and failed again. Back in Apia, the three powers had built up a fleet in the roadstead. The Germans and Americans had three warships each and the British one.

In 1889, just at the point when the rival navies were ready to begin shooting, a hurricane whipped in from the sea. Reluctant to pull out in the face of storm warnings, the captains elected to stay and watch each other until it was too late. When the full force of the hurricane struck, only the British ship *Calliope* was able to beat out through the passage, while the American and German ships were pushed on to the reef. The crew of the *Trenton* lined the deck and cheered the *Calliope*. Many of the American sailors who were cheering must have known that within a short time they would be wrecked and fighting for their lives, but in the spirit of the moment they saluted the seamanship of their comrades. As it was the Americans lost fifty-four men and the Germans ninety-two.

For a time the hurricane averted hostilities between the three powers, but not between the Samoan factions. The Europeans living in Apia grew tired of the kingship squabbles and set up a municipality. Malietoa Talavou and Laupepa continued their struggle, however, and yet another claimant to the throne appeared in the person of the Tui A'ana Tamasese, who was crowned at Leulumoega. Once more a naval ship intervened and the interested parties agreed to Laupepa assuming the crown with Tamasese becoming the "vice king"— probably the only one in history. But even this arrangement did not survive for long. The next move came from the Germans, who deposed Laupepa because he continued to press for British or American annexation. This gave Josefa Mata'afa, another principal title-holder, a chance to contend for power. He refused the crown from the Germans, however, as he did not wish to become their pawn, but the "vice king" Tamasese accepted. Laupepa went into exile.

The Germans now established a strict order and promulgated regulations which made them and their king unpopular. Failure to pay tax, for instance, meant deportation for the village leaders. Apia people joined Mata'afa to protest. The Germans replied by sending a naval squadron to bombard Mata'afa's headquarters on Manono. The old chief shrewdly realised that he could do little against the Germans, but much against their Samoan supporters. In September 1889 he asked for the borders of the Apia Municipality to be clearly marked, and then began a battle against the king just outside the town. It was a gruesome, grizzly fight which raged for three days around the municipality, with warriors emerging from the bush to wave severed heads. Tamasese's German Premier, Herr Brandeis, appealed to Mata'afa to stop the war, and when the chief refused sent a punitive force against him. Mata'afa beat this force.

An uneasy peace was restored, but Mata'afa failed to get the kingship on his terms due to German opposition. Laupepa returned from exile, assumed the title and the Germans then seized Mata'afa and sent him into exile.

When Laupepa died a new struggle for succession developed between Malietoa Tanumafili and Mata'afa. The issue was discussed by a law court, which ruled in favour of Tanumafili. Displeased, the Germans closed it, and now set Mata'afa up as king. The British and American consuls then had a party from their warships reopen the court, which ratified Tanumafili as King. But Mata'afa, having finally obtained the crown, refused to give it up. Eight days later he attacked the forces of Tanumafili and won. Tanumafili resigned and at last the three powers agreed to divide the islands of Samoa between them. Britain was to take Savai'i, Germany Upolu, and the United States Tutuila and Manu'a. Britain declined her share in favour of the cession of German claims to land in Tonga, the Solomon Islands and West Africa. Thus Germany got both Savai'i and Upolu.

The Germans very quickly imposed a no-nonsense Teutonic order, but in Tutuila the theoretically anti-colonial Americans did not quite know what to do. They had no colonial machinery, and President McKinley declared this territory the responsibility of the Department of Navy. Commander B.F. Tilley made the issue formal by accepting a Deed of Cession from all the principal chiefs except the Tui Manu'a, who refused. Tui Manu'a finally did sign—five years after the event—but he did so solely to obtain privileges for his people.

American Samoa became officially American on 17 April 1900, when the flag of the United States was raised on the knoll, Muaga o ali'i, where at present the Governor's Mansion is located. Since then 17 April has been a public holiday, which the Samoans in their fashion have turned into a spectacle no visitor can forget.

In Western Samoa, the political situation changed dramatically at the outbreak of the First World War. A New Zealand contingent landed and arrested the German nationals. After the war New Zealand took over the administration of the territory under mandate from the League of Nations, only to find that the Samoan people had lost none of their pride or desire for independence. The spirit of the times was reflected in the Mau movement.

The New Zealand administration, clumsy if essentially humane, did not deal with the Samoans in the heavy-handed German fashion. Instead, they took half-measures, first offering hope for something better and then pulling back in the face of demands. Samoan leaders were exiled. In 1929, a mass demonstration by the Mau developed into a riot. The New Zealand soldiers panicked and killed eleven Samoans, including the High Chief Tamasese, whose ancestors had figured so prominently in the history of their country. A warship arrived and a naval party went out to arrest the leaders of the Mau. Only the election of a new Government in New Zealand in 1935 eased the situation. The new Government released O.F. Nelson, the leader of the Mau, from exile and paid his fare home. The Samoans were then given a greater share in government. From this point on relations between the two countries continued to improve until in 1962 New Zealand relinquished all control and Western Samoa became an independent nation.

WESTERN SAMOA

THE ADMINISTRATIVE CENTRE of Western Samoa is Apia. Inevitably the visitor goes there first. Apia is steeped in history. Graves of former kings rest among the palms of Mulinuu at the westernmost point of Apia Harbour. The *fono* (meeting house) for the Samoan Parliament is located here, along with the Lands and Titles Court, Broadcasting House, and the Apia Observatory. Palms cast their dappled shade on the neat lawns. In the lagoon, which is very wide at this point, fish traps run at all angles and the small *faleo'o*, from which watchmen wait for the schools of mullet, dot the shallows.

The road sweeps along the verge of the lagoon, east towards Beach Road, the main thoroughfare of Apia. You pass the historic Casino Hotel, a fading relic of German imperialism, past the new markets and on into the heart of the commercial section. At Christmas time a belt of flamboyants sparkles red from the markets as far as the Returned Servicemen's Association Club. Then the road widens out again until you reach the bridge across the Mulivai River just past the Catholic Cathedral. It is a long sweep from Mulinuu to Pilot Point at Matautu. If you should happen to want to walk the distance, then Aggie Grey's is sure to lure you in for a cold beer or as good a *citron pressé* as you'll get in Tahiti or Noumea, but make sure you ask for it as a fresh lemonade. Aggie's is a famed hostelry. It is one of the famous hotels of the South Pacific and Aggie herself, a charming woman, is almost a legend.

James A. Michener wrote a good deal about the Pacific and some of his work, publicised through theatre and films, has added to the lure of the South Seas. In his story, *Tales from the South Pacific*, Michener wrote of "Bloody Mary" and there are those who will say that Aggie was its model. Nothing could be further from the truth. But Aggie does have a fund of stories of her own, including that of her rise as a business entrepreneur.

During the height of the G.I. invasion during the war against Japan in the Pacific, Aggie ran a hamburger bar and quickly became a favourite with the visiting troops because of her good humour and good looks. She has raised a big family, but only her son Alan has elected to stay in Apia to look after the family business. Today, he and his attractive wife Marina look after the hotel and the family store next to it. Alan is quiet and reticent, but his shyness is more than compensated for by Aggie, who mixes with the guests throughout the day and passes on some of her stories. Alan prefers to retreat into a sailing boat at the weekends. An able yachtsman, he represented Western Samoa at the South Pacific Games in Port Moresby.

Sometimes yachts swing at anchor in the roadstead outside the hotel, much as the warships used to do in the olden days. Big liners, however, can now tie up at the wharf near Pilot Point. The days of lightering have gone forever. To deepen the berth, dredges sucked up tons of bottom and dumped it in a wide reclamation which juts into the harbour just in front of the Returned Servicemen's Association.

An old Samoan legend claimed that as long as the wreck of the German warship, the *Adler*, which was driven on to the reef in the 1889 hurricane, was left undisturbed, there would be no hurricane damage in Samoa. In 1966, fill from the dredge finally covered the last remains of the *Adler* and within days the first major hurricane for about fifty years whipped in, leaving a trail of destruction in town, villages and plantations.

Probably the best time to visit Apia is during the first week of June, when the nation hurls itself with enthusiasm into its best *fiafia* (celebration). The country regained its independence on New Year's Day in 1962, but because the weather is better in June, the annual Independence Day Celebrations are held at that time.

If you chance to arrive then, as some do, without knowing the reason for it all, the atmosphere will immediately infect you. Lots of people are moving about the town day and night. Stalls are being set up along Beach Road. Huge bundles of sugar cane, thick and juicy, are piled up in front. Various contingents are practising marching. The day starts bright and even before dawn people are moving towards Mulinuu. It is here that the flag will be raised, the speeches made and the parade reviewed. Then on into town for dancing, song and sports contests. That night Apia becomes one huge club. Anyone with suitable premises can hang out a sign, but there are a few favourites such as the RSA, a businessman's resort. This club is a favourite of Emilio Fabricious, himself the owner of a club with one of the most magnificent names you'll find in the world: Emilio's By The Harbour Light Boogie House. On the sign there is a sketch of a lighthouse along with the title. Hula Town, an old Pacific favourite, is no more, but the Sunset Club next door continues on its merry way.

The Sunset Club is one of many that suddenly made their appearance on the Apia scene, but it has persisted. There's the Apia Club, still withstanding the test of time; Emilio's, backed by his trading store, Mount Vaea, a hardy night spot, and the Surfside, which styles itself a discotheque. The Surfside steals the scene these days. Peace corps representatives, United Nations men on various jobs in Samoa, New Zealanders in "seconded" positions and the intelligentsia of Apia usually find their way here during some part of Saturday night.

The second day of the Independence Celebrations begins before dawn. Thousands of people head quietly for Beach Road. Some have waited there all night. Today is *fautasi* day, when the great longboats with some fifty men each will race in over a distance of five miles from the open sea, to cross the finishing line in front of the huge crowd. As the faint light of dawn lights up the scene you get the feeling that almost all of Samoa is here. We wait on the western tip of the wharf and listen to a transistor for the start of the race. A radio commentator is on the tug watching the line up. They're off! This year, a challenger from Pago Pago is competing. The Pago *fautasi*, named *Televise* (television), is a formidable challenger to the local boys. The boat was built in Western Samoa and raced successfully there before it was taken to Utulei in American Samoa. Soon, the commentary reveals that there's going to be a close struggle between *Televise* and *Matua*. They're neck and neck as they come through the opening in the reef. A mighty roar goes up from the people on Pilot Point and the wharf.

Matua! Alu! Alu! (Matua! Go! Go!)

Fo'ard a drummer beats the time Samoan style, on a biscuit tin. At the back the cox, facing the rowers, signals. As they pass the tip of the wharf where we stand still neck and neck, the strain increases. The white blades of the long oars flash in the early sun, and the muscled backs bend to the weight. Sweat bands on foreheads keep their eyes clear. The people yell, among them relatives who might well be thinking of the $500 prize. They flash past and cover the last hundred yards in seconds. The oars of *Televise* go up in salute—a triumph for the visitors. The first time a visiting team from Pago has won a *fautasi* race in Western Samoa in some forty years.

Later the whaleboat and *paopao* (canoe) races are held but are less exciting. People chew their sugar cane and chat in the warm sun. How could *Televise* beat the local boys? About noon the triumphant crew, two abreast and swollen with pride, march along Beach Road to receive their prize.

The last outstanding spectacle for the visitor, unless he happens to be interested in athletics and Rugby, is the race meeting at Apia Park. The only race meeting in the world, as Bob Shaffer from California observed, where it is possible to pick a winner by his looks. The good horses are so obviously superior in looks that the decision is made relatively easy. True, the jockeys are an unknown quantity, but these little riders, some only nine

16

years old, pound round the course with deadly intent. Between times a brass band keeps things lively and should you feel like refreshments and have a set of your own teeth, you might try chewing sugar cane. The type grown in Samoa was brought there centuries ago by the first early settlers. Most family plantations grow it and most Samoans enjoy it. The juice is refreshing and the effect on teeth is magnificent.

For a look at the rest of Apia the visitor would be wise to seek expert help. Anna Stencill of Aggies or Jane Ah Vai of Retzlaffs, a local trading firm, I found very helpful. They know the place inside out and have the added advantage of being very attractive and intelligent. Inevitably on the list is Vailima, the residence built by Robert Louis Stevenson and now occupied by the Head of State. The building, some three miles back from the beach, is set in lovely grounds under the shade of Mt Vaea. Stevenson lived here only a short time. When he died the Samoans, who recognised him as a great man, carried his body to the top of Mt Vaea where it lies to this day with his epitaph on the side of the limestone tomb:

> Under the wide and starry sky,
>   Dig my grave and let me lie,
> Glad did I live and gladly die,
>   And I laid me down with a will.
> This be the verse you grave for me;
>   Here he lies where he longs to be,
> Home is the sailor, home from the sea,
>   And the hunter home from the hill.

Even in the short time that he spent in Samoa Stevenson went on with his craft. His story "The Beach at Falesa" is one of the most stirring South Sea adventures yet written. He described it as a piece which got closer to the essence of Samoa than anything he had done before.

If you mean to toil up to Stevenson's grave, you'll be advised to do so early in the morning before it gets too hot. The trail is often steep and sometimes slippery. It is not a very high climb and even someone who is not fit can probably get there in an hour and a half. The trail that begins at the foot of the hill goes past the swimming pool that Stevenson had made in the Vailima Stream.

I have often wondered how RLS came to be buried on top of one of the spurs of Mt Vaea. Stevenson was only forty-nine when he collapsed and died without warning one evening. The next day a party of thirty Samoans cleared a ten-foot-wide path to Tia Sooala, the spot where the burial was to take place, and there cleared an area. At noon the body was placed in a coffin and carried to the top, with Stevenson's wife and mother following. Samoan friends, including a number of chiefs, and members of the European community made up the train. At the top the Rev. W.E. Clarke read the Church of England service and the Rev. J.E. Newell, according to the *Samoa Herald*, "gave an eloquent address in Samoan".

Stevenson's wife died in 1914, in California. She was cremated and her ashes were brought to Apia the following year by her daughter. Again a party of Europeans and Samoans made the ascent to Tia Sooala, where her urn was wrapped in fine mats and interred in the tomb.

Stevenson's love for his wife was profound, and at last the woman of whom he had written:

> Teacher, tender comrade, wife,
>   A fellow farer true to life,
> Heart whole and soul free,
>   The August Father gave to me.

came to join Tusitala in his chosen resting place.

There are several other spots, such as the sliding rock at Papaseea, which have attracted visitors for a long time. Somerset Maugham has these rocks figuring in one of his stories. The flow of the water has smoothed a corridor in the lava rock. When you sit in it, the force of the flow builds up and then shoots you down with some velocity. The girls from the tour offices will take you through plantations and explain in detail everything about cocoa beans, bananas, coconuts, taro or anything else you ask about. They will also drive you past Lepea Village, where the Prime Minister's house is a unique example of the blending of Samoan design and European materials.

The Samoans are deeply religious and fastidious in their observance of the Sabbath. Visitors must be careful to cause no offence.

THE COUNTRYSIDE

Geologically Western Samoa is a young country. The land mass was formed through the flow of lava from volcanic eruptions out of the limitless Pacific Ocean. Volcanic activity is still going on. The last eruption occurred in 1911, when lava poured out of the crater of Mt Matavanu in Savai'i, destroying all that lay in its path except for the grave of a virgin girl. Tourists now stop here to shake their heads in wonder. The volcanic soil is very fertile and this, combined with ample rainfall, makes the islands a lush garden. The mountains, which rise up to just over 6,000 feet in Savai'i, are jungle-clad.

Ferns, convolvulus, reeds, and bamboo make the tropical rain forest almost impenetrable, but the effect from the roadside is one of beauty. Down the slopes towards the sea there is usually a thin belt of flat land which gives way to a lagoon. For the most part the villages are close to the sea. There is an ample village common of well-trimmed grass and round this are the *fales*. Churches dominate the buildings and contrast their huge limestone walls against the open sides of the thatched huts. A visitor gets his first unforgettable experience during his drive in from the airport at Faleolo to Apia. The road winds through the settlements, past the palms and groves of banana. The tourist can watch the changing style of the *fales*, some rounded, some oval, some high on mounds of lava rock. There are patches of *taro* and the huge *ta'amu;* cocoa beans drying on mats in the hot sun; washing hung on hedges of hibiscus. But most fascinating are the people. The Samoans are golden-skinned, bright-eyed and physically superb. There may be a game of cricket or Rugby practice, canoes moving in the lagoon, or perhaps a fish drive. There are sure to be people swimming in pools made in the streams, or taking a shower under the village tap. There is no self-consciousness and the visitor's curious gaze will be met with open, laughing eyes.

In my previous travels round Samoa I had stayed at villages, a necessity when moving with an official *malaga* (tour). Now, I was going somewhere remote, alone with my cameras. The spot I chose after talking to Jane at Retzlaffs was a village at Aleipata, on the eastern tip of Upolu. There was a tour going out on Sunday and I joined the party.

The road east from Apia gives you the impression that you are going back into time. The villages look progressively less opulent, and the countryside is a good deal more rugged. There are scenic points en route such as the falls at Falega and Fuipisia. A slight diversion also gives you a look at Fagaloa Bay and the drive over the mountains leading up to Mafa Pass is stimulating enough for you to ignore the bumps. Once out on the west coast, you are in different country. The lagoons tend to be confined and exceptionally clear. Many of the villages nestle on clean white sand. It is good country for the *palolo*, but more of this later.

It is noon when the tour car stops at the village of Ulutogia. This is one of three villages facing the big lagoon with the islands of Nu'utele and Nu'ulua beyond. For the most part the *fales* perch on lava foundations built up on white sand. *Fale laititi* (little houses is the

18

literal translation, but it means toilets) jut out into the lagoon. We passed the stream and the swimming pool and when the car stops, children and young girls come running up. We have found the house of Peta Talataiga and the tour girl explains that Jane would like the family to look after me for a few days so I can get some pictures. Without any fuss my cases are taken out of the car, but before I can follow them to the *fale* I'm surrounded.

"What is your name? Are you married? How many children? Where do you come from? How long are you staying?"

Peta's housegirl, Siaivao, chases them away and leads me in. Peta, who used to work in Apia, speaks English. She laughs at me. After all, why would anyone, particularly a *palagi* (white man) want to come to Aleipata and live in a *fale* when he could be comfortable in a hotel in Apia? The logic is hard to deny and the fact that I choose to do so makes me a curiosity. Peace corps, people say. *Leai* (No) reply those who know. A *tusitala* (story teller) then. But this has a presumptuous ring to it. After all, Stevenson had the title.

I get my cameras and prepare for a walk. Lemafoe, Peta's niece, comes over and exercises her school English. She speaks it well, with a delightful syntax and scores off Siaivao who cannot speak it and whose shyness makes it even more difficult. The three of us set out, walking towards Vailoa, the girls eagerly carrying my cameras and handing out information to the *palagi*. It is nice to walk after the long ride from Apia. Strange, but it takes less time to fly from Pago to Auckland in a direct flight than it does to go from Apia to Aleipata. A tribe of kids join us at every *fale* and even the determined efforts of the big girls cannot get rid of them. On the way back we buy some sugar cane, much to the envy of the five-to-eight-year-olds who follow us. At three o'clock in the afternoon we attend the LMS church next door. That night everyone goes *ta'afao* (walkabout)—it's a Sunday special in Samoa.

Some of the folk who are related to Peta's husband talk to me. They invite me to visit their plantations and to go fishing with them. At this point I wish I could speak Samoan. People come around to Peta's and we talk in the light of the Tilly lamp, Lemafoe acting as the interpreter. Peta's little boy has got used to me to the extent that he now comes up and points demandingly at my food. I spend the night on a western-style bed, covered with a kapok mattress—the kapok picked in the village and prepared there. The sides of the *fale* are open to the south-east trades, so that I can see past the dark shapes of the palms right into the lagoon, where more than a mile away the surf booms phosphorescent on the reef.

We have our breakfast and to make sure Peta is not out of pocket because of my stay, I press some money on her. She takes it that I would like *palagi* food although this is not stated. It is only at lunchtime that this becomes obvious. Siaivao has been to the store and there is a host of cans. Everything has been opened and placed in front of me. I eat Samoan-style, sitting cross-legged and Siaivao sits opposite fanning me. If ever a system was designed to make a man feel like a king, this must be it. When I have finished the women eat what is left.

"What do you eat for breakfast, Peta?"

"Taro or breadfruit and tea."

"Lunch?"

"Taro or breadfruit".

"Dinner?"

"Taro and breadfruit and fish and coconut cream."

I was there long enough to see that sometimes there's chicken too. It depends on the family; those who have the means usually lavish it on food.

It is great work taking pictures at Aleipata, particularly of the people because they are so willing. After the first two days I have taken so many my film is beginning to run out. But people insist. They come from the end of the village to pose and listen for the slap of the reflex mirror. When it goes off they smile and say *uma*—it is finished. In the evening I put on my *lavalava* and in the gathering dusk, walk down for my bath. As in the morning, this attracts considerable attention. The water is cool and velvet soft. Above me, a few stray clouds from Tutuila rise up in a contorted column. Night suddenly descends and I walk back to my *fale* in the dark.

Peta is pregnant and due to have a baby in a month. She does nothing, but it does not make her happy. She sits, talks to friends and takes her afternoon nap. Life is no good, she says. It is making her lazy. She wants to go back to Apia, where she can get a job.

Next day, in the bush I talk to planters Lipau, Pele and Ulu'uala. They don't like their lot. We drink fresh coconuts and I tell them they're living in paradise.

"No," says Ulu'uala. "We have no money. We want to go to New Zealand, get work, earn money, have good clothes, buy a car and eat nice food."

"You're crazy. I come here to envy you and you envy me."

Tauaga Tulia is twenty-one years old, married, and as fine a man as you would meet anywhere. He is also an excellent fisherman, who supplies Peta's family with their seafood. Tauga speaks no English, but he knows I want to go fishing. When the tide is good, Tauga says so. He has his home-made goggles, shanghai and the sharpened steel rod. His *paopao* is in good order. Other men, some with tattooed flanks, are walking down to the beach. A conch shell has called them up. The *paopaos* begin heading east, to assemble near the reef. Each man, confident and relaxed, skims his craft to the meeting point. Some twenty canoes draw up. I look at the fishermen intently. Fine men each one, some with long hair tied at the back. The most striking individual is the man with the conch shell. Black from the sun, he has the look of a man who knows all about nature and cares for little else. He raises the shell and sounds a long blast. No one says anything, but the *paopaos*, now in line, begin to race away with the wings forming a half-moon. Finally they close up into a wide circle, and the men beat the water and rattle the sides of their canoes with paddles. At a point when the circle is fairly small the conch sounds again. Anchors go over the side and the men follow them.

The first plunge I watch from my canoe. The water is exceptionally clear and the divers are visible as they search for the fish they have driven to hide in the coral. You see a man aim and fire, come up with a small fish on his spear, bite it on the head to kill it, string it up, and go down again. Nothing except poisonous fish are spared. Eels, octopus, crabs, shellfish and other fish are taken, and after some ten minutes, when the area is considered empty, up they come. Many are already eating some of the fish they have caught.

Lelei (good) says Tauaga, offering me one to eat raw. I elect to have it later, cooked.

It was to be my last night at Ulutogia. The *matai* of the family and his brother were with us for dinner, which with my contribution seemed like a feast. We ate well and washed it down with Samoan cocoa.

I was to catch a bus for Apia at three o'clock the next morning. That night, a visiting concert party was playing at Vailoa and a group of us went to see it. The programme was a presentation of three one-act plays. The first was *Puss in Boots;* the second about Rohsoni the American millionaire and the third, complete with a magnificent scaffold, the tale of how an innocent joke can have nasty consequences. The people loved it. The play was staged in the open air in a grove of breadfruit trees, with the spectators sitting or standing on the grass. Tilly lamps on tall stakes lit the scene.

A feature of the performance was the range of costumes used by the players. The first two plays were comedies and had the desired effect. Samoans love humour and find it easy to laugh, but the last play ended with a dramatic hanging on the rickety scaffold. A live man is hoisted. He hangs by a carefully concealed brace, but for those who don't know, it looks as if the noose round his neck is having its effect. As he is hoisted up, he kicks and twists and slowly expires.

There was no call for me at three o'clock next morning. Peta said everyone had slept in, but I felt there had been a conspiracy. There was to be no bus the next morning, so I would have to wait. Seeing my carefully drawn schedules had gone to the winds, there was only one thing to do—enjoy my two extra days at Ulutogia. I swam, walked as far as Amaile and even made an attempt to get out to the islands of Fanuatapu and Namu'a.

The next night a group from our village went to Malaela for an evening at the movies. It was a double feature. The first one, a Western, had lost synchronisation between picture and sound, but it made little difference. The people, sitting on the floor, wanted action. The next was a war film, and equally acceptable. It is a three-mile walk from Malaela to Ulutogia and our party, anxious for an early start in the morning, set a cracking pace. There are no cars here. Just the odd truck or bus which goes through. Otherwise, everyone walks— and what could be better?

I got to Apia some three days late—perhaps it was four. I don't know. Peta had no calendar and time had lost its meaning.

Viko Meisake of the Department of Economic Development and Jane Ah Wai proposed a *malaga* to the other end of the island. There was to be a church dedication at Falelatai, and then we would double back, go over the mountains and visit Lefaga, one of the most picturesque spots in Samoa. It was here that Gary Cooper was filmed in *Return to Paradise*. We bought *palusami* and *niu* (drinking nuts) at the markets and set off.

In Samoa the observance of custom makes heavy demands on the people and a church dedication is an event of great importance. Churches can only be built by community effort, followed by a good deal of communal pride. Pastors, dignitaries associated with the village, and relatives pour in from everywhere. They bring mounds of food and fine mats which will be presented and redistributed in a ritual which goes back to the start of Samoan history.

The sun is shining hot, but the *matai* of the village, stripped to the waist as tradition demands, are toiling among the heaps of taro, kegs of salt beef and cases of pilchards. Fat pigs, part-roasted, rest on carrying braces. A band, the brass polished till it burns, plays outside the church, and people mill about in a great throng. The service finishes, the church is consecrated, and the dignitaries in Sunday white, clutching their Samoan Bibles, pour out into the heat and strike their umbrellas. Now begins the distribution of food; first, the quota is allocated for each family and then the family distributes to each member.

We leave the village and stop in the shade of palms on a strip of beach facing the island of Manono and eat our *palusami* and *taro* and then wash it down with fresh drinking nuts.

The road to Lefaga turns off at Laulumoega and climbs over a saddle to the south-west coast. It is an easy road. We stopped briefly at Lefaga and then went on to Salamumu for a swim before heading back over the new road to Apia. Before we parted, Viko and I made arrangements to go fishing for *palolo* during their rise on one night of October.

As a parting shot I said: "Viko, we'll have to take some models for our fishing."

I was staying with Peter Creevey and his wife Lagi. They elected to go. So did Momoe Malietoa and Sia Moimoi. The problem of models was solved as well as good company to eat the *palolo*, once we caught it. Viko's wife and Lagi made the nets and the *ula* (necklaces of flowers and fragrant herbs) which would ensure success with the *palolo*. Creevey consulted the experts as to the precise night when the *palolo* were to rise and all arrangements were completed.

There was once a great deal of mystery about the *palolo*. In fact it is a string of spawn cast off by a shy little annelid which lives buried in the coral. It comes up on one night of the year in long threads of green ova and brown sperm. The threads rise up twisting and

21

moving as if they were worms. They come up in clusters, some over a foot long, to be scooped gently by eager fishermen. The *palolo* rise just before dawn and then, as the sun comes up from the east and lights up the water, the *palolo* dissolve into an oily smudge. The microscopic ova and sperm mingle and settle into the coral to begin a new cycle.

Viko arrived at the Creevey's at three o'clock in the morning. Sia and Momoe came shortly after. We stowed food, cameras and cushions and began the stiff climb up Vailima Road to the west coast. Viko's pickup sparked and missed and lost power up the steep drag, requiring Viko to stop for adjustments. We went over the top in good style, confident of reaching our appointed fishing spot. As we drove on the first light of dawn began to streak the sky from the east. Stark kapok trees and huge banyans mingled with the palms along the roadside. The stars still shone bright in the deep blue as the first brush of pink began to line the dome of the sky. Flying foxes by the score and in all shapes and sizes moved slowly above, heading for their roosting places.

When we got to Lotofaga there were many people already in the lagoon. It seemed the *palolo* were on. Not so. It was a false alarm and a number of reputations were sure to suffer. Perhaps the next day would be the day.

Thus we found ourselves on the road again the following morning. Much of the charm and excitement had gone and there was a shower or two of rain as well, but this time the *palolo* were definitely on. Our party went into the lagoon before dawn and I waited for sufficient light to take my photos. A great number of people were silently at work scooping *palolo*.

The lagoon here is narrow and a great surf was booming on the barrier reef, sending small waves hissing among the fishermen. Most people were putting the catch into pouches carried for the purpose; others had containers in canoes into which they were dumping their catch. Whole families were working the lagoon, waist-deep in water. Our party dispersed like well-trained cormorants and began scooping *palolo*. There was a huge bank of clouds to the east, blocking the sun. It robbed me of light, but the effect was breathtaking. As the sun rose, it began to send shafts of light through gaps in the clouds, turning the lagoon crimson and lighting up the fishermen.

I took my pictures quickly, put away my cameras and joined our party, but before they would let me fish, I had to eat a mouthful of *palolo*. It wriggled in my mouth and then dissolved to leave a tangy, fresh taste. You can keep your caviar, I thought, and went to it with a will. Between us we caught quite a lot of *palolo* and purchased some more before going back. At the Creevey's we had some cooked for breakfast and agreed to meet that night with others for a celebration dinner, a great feast with German sparkling Trocken wine to complement the *palolo*.

The *palolo* plays an important part in Samoan life, perhaps because it appears but once in the year. Families living near good *palolo* areas use it to wipe clean their social obligations.

SAVAI'I

Savai'i is the great island of Samoa. It is the largest island; it possesses the highest mountains and because it is relatively free of Western influence, it is the most exciting for a visitor. I had been to Savai'i previously, but my new *malaga* was to prove the most memorable. During the Independence Celebrations I met Rob Shaffer and Larry Hansen, two Peace Corps boys from California. Rob's parents were on a visit to Apia, and I learned that they were to go to Savai'i to Rob's village and stay there for a few days visiting his Samoan *aiga* (family). Here was a chance to photograph something different and the Shaffers were delighted. We left Apia early for the wharf at Mulifanua, just west of the airport. Small ferries make the one-hour run over the fifteen miles of water to Salelologa. This one was crammed with people returning from the festivities and it was just as well we got there early as some had to be left behind. At Salelologa a bus took us the few miles to Iva, where Magele and his family were waiting. We drank 'ava (kava) and Rob Shaffer senior thanked his host:

"Thanks be to God we have arrived safely to visit with you. We have come to thank you for taking care of our boy. . . ."

Rob teaches at Iva and Larry Hansen, who was also with us, teaches at Fagamalo. There was to be a full programme for the three days the Shaffers were to spend at the village. In the afternoon, as Rob and his parents had a number of things to talk about with Magele, Larry and I took our spearguns and joined some fishermen. We went out to the barrier reef and saw some big fish, but it was impossible to get close enough. Back at the village the eighteen members of Magele's clan, plus a number of local matai had met Rob's parents. They prepared a huge feast, but first the Shaffers had to go to the village pool for their bath. This, in Samoa, is a public affair. Instructed in advance on the proper mode of behaviour, his parents went down to the pool. Mrs Shaffer went in among the women while Rob's father dipped into the large pool reserved for men. There's an art in washing yourself in public in Samoa. It is made relatively easy by using a lavalava, under which you can scrub yourself without disrobing. A mob of kids stood off at a safe distance and laughed at the antics of the papalagi. The Shaffers for their part played up their role.

In correspondence with their son the Shaffers had learnt details of each member of the family. They had learnt each member's approximate size and when they finally arrived at Iva, they brought two cases of clothes as presents. For Magele there was a handsome wrist watch. It was wonderful to see the surprise of each member of the clan as the gifts were called—there was even one for Pacifica, the latest addition to the clan.

But perhaps the most touching part of the visit was an undertaking given by the Shaffers to Magele that they would take his granddaughter Va'aipu for a year to the States for additional education. A bright, attractive girl of sixteen, Va'aipu was thrilled.

Next day being Sunday we went to the lofty church at Iva, where Va'aipu was the envy of her friends in her smart new dress. In the afternoon the Shaffers had a bus arranged for a trip to the falls and pool at Letolo, where we had a picnic lunch and swam for several hours. The Shaffers finished their visit to Iva with a bus trip to Fagamalo, where Larry teaches. I stayed with Larry for a couple of days' diving and then caught a small boat directly for Apia.

STATISTICS

Western Samoa is one of the smallest independent nations in the world. It lies between 13 degrees and 15 degrees south of the equator and between longitude 171 and 173. The total land area is just over 1,100 square miles and it supports a population of approximately 150,000. Samoa has one of the highest birth rates in the world. There are only a few Europeans but no other ethnic group.

The family system is patriarchal and socialistic. Each family elects its "head" who is known as a matai. His job is to see that the affairs of the extended family unit are administered properly, that the land is fairly divided and the produce equally shared. He protects his unit's territory and adjudicates in family disputes. He sits on the village council and depending on the status of his title, exercises his role there.

There is no universal voting system in Samoa. The constitution provides that only bearers of matai titles will vote for the representatives of the Legislative Assembly which constitutes the Samoan Parliament. There has been, in elections past, a sudden proliferation of matai titles in areas where campaigning is critical. The system has found acceptance, but Samoans would not be known as the Irish of the Pacific without good reason and it is unlikely that the Government will continue to exist long under the present constitution without some attempt being made to change it.

The Head of State, at present Malietoa Tanumafilii II, is the chief executive through the powers vested in his office. In fact, he does not exercise this power except through ratification of laws approved by the Legislative Assembly. He also appoints the Prime Minister, who must, however, have the confidence of the Assembly. With the Prime Minister, he appoints eight members from the Assembly who will constitute the Cabinet, and the Executive Council of which he is a member. The Constitution provides that the next Head of State shall be elected for a term of five years and it is understood that the candidate will be chosen from one of the four princely families of Samoa.

Let us place a hibiscus flower behind our ear
Its smile will light our face.

The coral reef shelters both the myriad fish and the land that lies beyond. A view looking west past Leone, on Tutuila.

Heading for Aleipata. Fragrant and lush, Samoa's rich countryside is one of the most fertile in the world. It is a young country in terms of geology and the lava flows from the volcanoes gives it a lunar appearance.

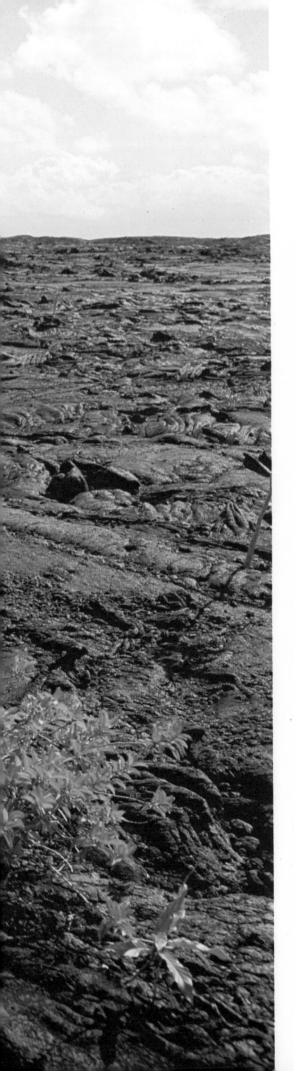

It is this lava which gives Samoa its wealth. The rich minerals flung up in the molten volcanic rock bestow upon the land an astonishing fertility. The lava field here on Savai'i, not far from Fagamalo, was deposited in an eruption in 1912, but already plants are breaking through and establishing themselves on the thick crust which in places is up to ten feet deep.

OVERLEAF

One of the most striking sights in Samoa is the layout of the villages and the construction of *fales*. They stand proudly on their piles of lava rock, their sides open to the clean, cooling breeze, their families gregarious and sociable. Some villages nestle round ample greens, dappled by palms and breadfruit trees, kapoks, hibiscus, frangipani and sugar cane. Others are pitched alongside lagoons, the *fales* on the very lip of the water. There's even a village built around the cone of an old volcano.

In Samoa even the European-sawn planks and iron roofing succumb to the Samoan touch. They are bent, moulded and fashioned by old master craftsmen who guard their reputations as jealously as the men who build the skyscrapers of New York.

Freddy's (*top right*) near Tafuna in American Samoa, is the latest example of how the old and the new can blend together without aesthetic or cultural offence.

No book on Samoa would be complete without a picture or mention of the *Fale laititi* (the little house) sometimes known as the "observatory". American Peace Corps sanitation experts are working hard to make sure that it will pass from the scene, to be mourned by none but the sentimental.

People

In a burst of enthusiasm, while we were travelling from Faleolo to Apia, a tourist next to me said, "This is fantastic! The place is beautiful and look at those houses. Even the people look like natives!"

There was no offence meant, only amazement. Who could blame him. After Hawaii and Tahiti, or for that matter any other place in the Pacific, Samoa stands out as different, as more original and exciting.

The intoxicating sights and sounds of Samoa are real enough, but it is the people who add the final overpowering attraction.

We were just turning away from Lefaga—the place where *Return to Paradise* was filmed—when a line of school children appeared. They were barefoot, of course, and most wore only the red school *lavalava*, embellished with *ula* of seeds and flowers. Who can look at these people without a pang of envy, or refuse to call them beautiful?

The day of the beachcomber is gone. *Samoa mo Samoa* means Samoa for the Samoans. A few *papalagi* manage to live there and one of them is Peter Creevey, who is married to the charming girl opposite. Her name is Lagi (Heaven) and they have two children, Taki and Runa. Peter is the editor of the *Samoa Times* and although he talks of going back to his native New Zealand, Samoa, as said the wise *matai* Tuala, has spun her web about him. Tuala once told me, "If he stays here for three years he will never leave." Peter has stayed there now for six.

It is hard to hunt for Samoan faces with a camera, not because the people turn away, but because when they see you they smile. Getting a serious picture is almost impossible.

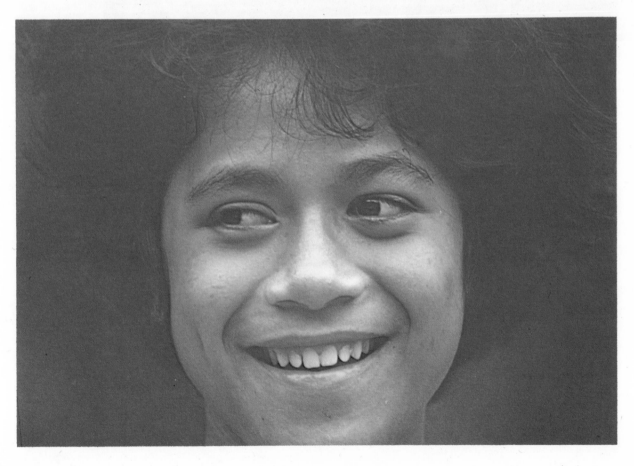

Jane Ahvai

Aggie Grey

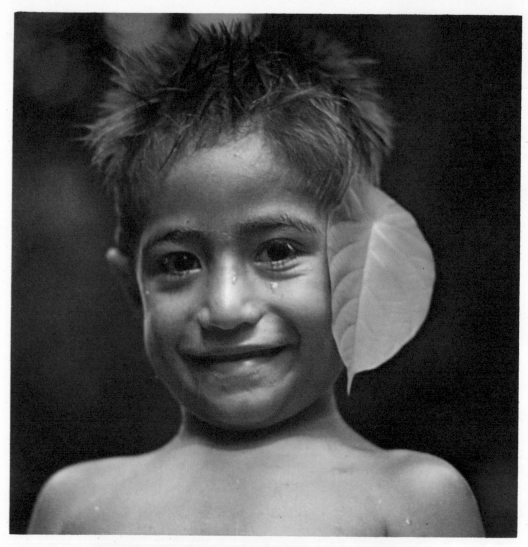

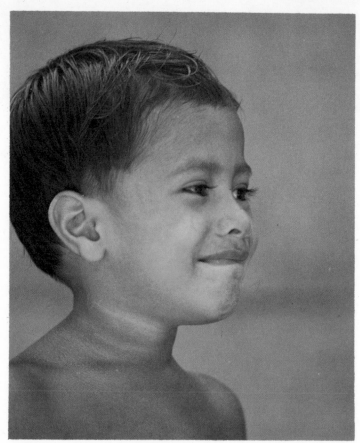

Their life consists of sunshine, swimming and song before the heavy hand of discipline molds them into shape.

Chande Drabble (*opposite top*) left Samoa as a child for California. She came back as a young woman for a holiday, married, and lives in American Samoa. She has faith in its future and only occasionally sighs for the fast, sophisticated life of the West Coast. Her husband, Tom, is a New Zealander, who drifted to Samoa on a contract job. Today, in partnership with a young American, John Newton, they run an expanding business.

Faces. Hats hide them, flowers decorate them.

Among the drums, flags and bunting, the Head of State (*above*) and the Prime Minister keep their eye on the first day of Western Samoa's Independence celebrations in 1969.

Matua alu! Alu! They shouted in my ear as the two great *fautasi* drew up. But *Televise* held the narrow margin.

Ever since the Samoans gave up war, they have played sport as if it was war!

One of the more unusual sights was this high jump specialist who went at the bar head first, somersaulting on the opposite side, to land on the ground on his back. I was unable to continue watching, but the crowd shared his pain and loved him for it.

The *talolo* and *suatai* (the rendering of food and fine mats) is one of the pillars of Samoan custom. At Leone, in American Samoa, the Director of the Office of Territories, Mrs Elizabeth Farrington (with glasses) and the Governor of American Samoa, John Haydon, and his wife, were the guests of the village.

In American Samoa there are two big events; Flag Day in April, which marks the cession of Tutuila and Manu'a to the United States, and the Fourth of July. The bands march, the flags are hoisted, there is singing and dancing.

The 'ava or _kava_ ceremony is still widely practised in Samoa. The 'ava precedes important ceremonial occasions, but is also served to tourists if they wish to learn something of this Samoan custom.

The serving of lavish food is a favourite Samoan pastime. Village fines are often exacted in food payments and no occasion of importance passes without a feast. Aggie Grey holds special nights when the best of Samoan fare is served.

Rupert Brooke spoke of the contrast between ballet and the Samoan *siva*. There is something about Samoan dancing which has long since gone from the formal disciplines of ballet. I watched a team of 200 youngsters from Manu'a performing at Fagatogo and shivers ran down my back. The exuberance, power and vitality under the hot sun; the colour and the oil and the complete involvement of the dancers was stirring.

The Samoans dance whenever they can and the *siva siva* is peculiar to their islands. It is danced on formal occasions; informally at cricket matches by those who suddenly feel in the mood, or at family entertainments or when a *malaga* has arrived. The Samoa Teachers' Training College (*above*) has one of the outstanding teams in Western Samoa. Overleaf, a knife dancer spins the *nifo oti* (teeth of death, as the knives are called) oblivious to the scorching heat.

94

Views of Apia (*left*) and Fagatogo. The shots of Apia were taken from the clocktower; Fagatogo is seen from the ridge above Solo Hill.

The Rainmaker Hotel, better known as the Pago Pago Intercontinental, was American Samoa's first attempt to attract tourists. Built with respect to Samoan style, it is one of the most attractive buildings in the South Pacific. *Opposite*, Robert Louis Stevenson's former home at Vailima, near Apia. The house, which is nearly 100 years old, has been enlarged and is now the official residence of the Head of State of Western Samoa. Stevenson's tomb rests on top of Mt Vaea, just behind the house.

The markets try to snare tourists with handicrafts which are both well-made and inexpensive. The huge roots are *ta'amu*, a coarse giant version of the *taro*.

The rise of the *palolo*. Dawn lights up canoes and people scooping up the "worms". *At right*, Momoe shows off some of her catch.

Diving at Fagamalo in Savai'i, I stalked the fisherman as he stalked his fish. *Above left* is the Crown of Thorns starfish. It lives by sucking out the live polyps of growing coral, slowly killing the reef. In some parts of the world, particularly on the Great Barrier Reef off Australia, it threatens the very existence of the reef.

There are many species of beautiful reef fish and fortunately a good number are considered inedible by Samoans, otherwise their existence would be in jeopardy. Someone once said that there are hundreds of ways of catching fish in Samoa because not one method is successful.

While the men dive and spear fish, the women are confined to more mundane tasks such as searching for shellfish or picking the spiny sea urchins. On shore their children are quick to smash and eat some.

If you happen to be up early enough you might see a lone fisherman casting into the surf beyond the reef. The waves seem to tower above him, but they stumble on the coral barrier.

The Peace Corps in Samoa. Larry Hansen and Rob Shaffer in a formal pose with Va'aipu in the village of Iva. The boys have volunteered for two years as teachers in Western Samoa.

I have never yet failed to be amazed by Samoan churches. It is not only the fact that they are so big and unusual, but there are so many of them. Imagine the labour that has gone into their building.

AMERICAN SAMOA

IT SO HAPPENED that Peter Creevey's office of the *Samoa Times* in Pago Pago required the services of a journalist. I offered to fill in until a suitable replacement could be found. My *fale* was a hurricane house at the village of Aua, owned by the family of Siafolao Leiato and his wife Ulopa. They had built it with the help of a Government loan, but found the closed walls not to their liking and retired next door to a dwelling more along the lines of *faa samoa* (the Samoan way). Siafolao and I soon became friends.

American Samoa is much smaller in area than its neighbour. The population, proportionately, is also small. There are some 28,000 Samoans living here, and, it is said, a number equally as large in Hawaii and the United States.

"We really screwed this place up," a tourist told me one day, and I noticed this breast-beating tendency among a number of Americans. Writing for the *Honolulu Advertiser* John Griffin has said:

"We divided the Samoas with Germany. Our goal was Pago Pago's great harbour for a coaling station. People called Samoans just happened to live there."

After its annexation the American naval station at Tutuila drifted on with little benefit to the people who had ceded their island. Then in 1961 the scene changed almost overnight. John F. Kennedy sent out Rex Lee as the new Governor with a brief directive: Clean the place up and get it moving. He got it moving. Tafuna airport, the road system, Lee Auditorium, the Intercontinental Hotel and the water reservoir systems were built in his time. He approved the controversial television education programme which reformed schooling in American Samoa and brought it sharply into world focus.

To make it work, he authorised the building of a television centre at Utulei and started building twenty-four elementary schools, which like the Intercontinental Hotel were artistically designed in Samoan style.

Lee's term transformed the little island and fired its people with new ambitions. When Owen Aspinall took over as Governor some reaction had set in. Difficulties were being experienced with the Reservoir system which was to end water shortage forever, the power generator tended to fail; television education was being questioned, and the new sewerage treatment plant at Utulei was getting little use; the Intercontinental Hotel and its Samoan shareholders were worried because there were insufficient rooms. Aspinall tried his best, but it was in encouraging Samoan political ambitions that he played his most important role.

Now power rests in the hands of John M. Haydon, a go-getting administrator from Seattle. He arrived with a full brief as to what needed doing and in his inaugural address spelled it out to the people. The country is once again on the edge of a new development period, but this time the Samoans are expected to have a much greater say in how it will be done and where the priorities will lie.

The political system in American Samoa is based on the Department of the Interior of Washington, which appoints the Governor (usually a political nominee) and then handles his demands, principally the budget. The office which deals with Samoa in the Department of the Interior deals with several other territories. It fights Samoa's case in Congress for Federal appropriations. Money generated locally is appropriated by the Samoan Legislature which consists of a Senate and a House of Representatives. The Senators are *matais* elected from each of the fourteen political countries and the seventeen representatives of the House are elected by universal adult suffrage.

The Governor, as head of the Executive, is responsible for the daily running of the

Territory. He meets with various departmental heads, approves projects and sometimes intervenes personally to get something moving. The Legislature is becoming more and more active. Since it began making laws in 1960, its scope has broadened and political awareness has mushroomed. Local people now have a good idea of what goes on and representatives such as Pita Sunia, a prominent member of the House of Representatives, have as good a nose as a bloodhound. They can be quick to call a house committee which gives them scope to examine public servants in as much detail as they like.

The third branch of the American Samoan Government is the judiciary, which consists of a High Court and District Courts. Criminal cases are prosecuted by the Attorney-General; defendants have recourse to a public defender should they desire one.

American Samoa, despite this American system of administration, is a no-status territory. Though the people have free access to the United States, they must apply for citizenship. This territorial status exempts Samoans from military service, yet on a per capita basis Samoans have one of the highest ratios of active service in Vietnam.

With growing political awareness, it has become accepted that a decision regarding the future of American Samoa must be made. A Political Status Commission is compiling a report on what it feels the future should be. There are several alternatives: independence, statehood, commonwealth status, union with Western Samoa, or the continuation of the present territorial system. Probably the Department of the Interior, which took over from the Navy in 1951, will continue to administer the Territory as long as the present system exists.

In comparison to its neighbour American Samoa is a rich country. The budget, combining local income of some US$5,000,000 with Federal appropriations of approximately US$10,000,000, pours a great deal of money into local hands. There are, one cynic observed, more motor vehicles than road—well, not quite, but Fagatogo is subject to motor jams. The two greatest employment agencies are the fish canneries and the Government. The canneries, situated on the eastern side of the Bay, rely on Japanese, Korean and Formosan fishermen to bring in the tuna they catch over a vast area of the Pacific. It is processed and canned with Samoan labour and exported to the United States duty-free. The canneries employ some 1,000 Samoans between them and there is a minimum wage. Fishing fleets which provision here also pour back a great deal of money.

The upshot of all this is that prices tend to be several times as high as in Western Samoa, with some joyful exceptions. The Government Store which imports all spirit and wine periodically has a sale, and during my stay I bought a crate of St Emilion 1962 which was being sold at just over a dollar a bottle, because the management felt it was getting too old.

The great jets which whisk people about at the speed of sound tend to make landfall at night, but if you happen to be lucky enough to come into Tafuna during the day, or steam into Pago Harbour in a good clear light, you are in for the first thrilling encounter. The jagged, bush-covered hills rush out to meet you and then as the road begins to skirt the bays from Nuuuli, the ocean breaks against the narrow reef in a pattern of ever-changing colours. Sometimes a fine spray hangs over the area, bathing your view in a soft, unreal light. Above to your left hang patches of *taro* on the steep slopes and the *fales* wink from among the palms and banana groves. The churches, as usual, tower above everything except the mountains.

Having passed the Flower Pot, a high rock just offshore at Niuloa Point, you enter the bay of Pago Pago and the most magnificent harbour in the South Pacific. A volcanic explosion of some magnitude formed this bay. It is deep enough, wide enough, and long enough to accommodate a fleet. The highest mountain, Mt Matafao, rises to over 2,000 feet on the left, and across the bay, offering their various faces as your taxi rolls along, are

122

Mt Alava and the Rainmaker (Mt Pioa). You have the feeling you are entering a huge canyon, and indeed, if the water was drained from the bay, this would be one of the most spectacular canyons in the world.

On past Fagalau, where the Lyndon Baines Johnson Tropical Medical Centre is situated, round Tulutulu Point and you come into the area known as Pago Pago. In fact this is the village of Utulei and on the neat little beach you will notice a house with fine shingles, keeping the weather off a *fautasi*. This is the victorious *Televise*, which won in Apia and which has also swept the stakes clean in Tutuila. On your left is the Lee Auditorium, and on the right, past Government houses, the striking design of the Pago Pago Intercontinental Hotel. Above the hotel, on Mauga-o-ali'i, stands the Governor's mansion, the Stars and Stripes fluttering briskly in the breeze with the tall palms for company.

Past this point begins Fagatogo, with the administrative buildings set round the *malae*. The trading stores are much as they've been for the past fifty years. Behind, *fales* and European-style houses rise from the jungle. The Bamboo Room, Pago Bar, and the Island Moon, are situated here. Across the *malae*, or village common, but only by the grace of temporary sanction, is the picture theatre, leading on from Centipede Road, the wharf and the Post Office. There are *fales* for the sale of handicrafts and on from them the new markets. The Governor's office and Court house are on the left as you leave the *malae* and some 200 yards onward, a new Max Haleck store rises on the site of the scene where Sadie Thomson and the Rev. Davidson had their confrontation in Somerset Maugham's short story *Rain*. Buildings continue on the left all the way to the apex of the bay. It is here that the true settlement of Pago Pago begins. This is in fact the biggest village in the Territory and the houses run back into the deep Vaitipo Valley. A sealed, twisting road creeps along the side and crosses into Fagasa, but the settlement here is small. There are more people crowded into communities round the bay. In front of Pago Pago a great reclamation has been completed with playing fields in a park and beautifully finished Samoan *fales* built for the tourist trade. The road continues on to the canneries, where visitors are welcome, and on to the east. It passes Aua, the village where I stayed, and on towards Breakers Point, which guards the eastern side of the bay.

The rain used to depress me when I first came to American Samoa. The deep bay and the structure of the mountains suck in moisture from the ocean to make this one of the wettest spots in the South Pacific. Often you can see it coming, marching resolutely. Mostly it comes in mild showers, but there are times when it thunders down in a tropical downpour so intense you cannot see ten yards ahead of you. The sky goes black and the roads become torrents of water. It is after such a downpour that Tutuila shows its most beautiful face to the visitor. As the sun comes out rainbows light up the bush and waterfalls cascade off steep cliffs. There are places in Tutuila which get more rain than others. My village of Aua, under the very brow of Mt Rainmaker, got more than its share, yet I was seldom wet.

In the business community the difference between Western and American Samoa is vast. On the village level it is not so obvious, except where the family has accepted a cash economy. Thus I was happy to see that my landlord Siafolao was well-versed in the way of his people.

"Siafolao," I asked him one Friday, "do you ever have *palusami*?"

"Sure," he replied, "you like it?"

So we planned a feast for the following Sunday.

Siafolao was up on Sunday before dawn. He was busy in his cookhouse and I saw him build up his *umu* (oven) which Samoans prepare from fist-size rocks. He arranged the stones carefully about faggots of wood and then fired the kindling. As the wood burnt the stones turned bright red and then white with heat. In the meantime Siafolao was patiently grating coconuts, the flesh of which, when reduced sufficiently, was squeezed through his hands with the aid of *fau* bark, until it became a rich cream. With the cream ready, he took a basket of young *taro* leaves, shaped them into a cup, poured a measure of coconut cream and some raw onion into it, and then closed the leaves up into a ball and wrapped this in turn in bigger leaves and then again in leaves of breadfruit. A pile of *taro*, the skins already scraped clean, lay on the side. When he had sufficient *palusami* prepared, the oven was ready. He took the stones aside and fanned away the ashes and embers with a banana leaf. Then he built up the sides and began arranging his *taro* among the hot rocks. Next he placed the packages of *palusami* and covered the oven with banana leaves. Over the top of this went some sacks and these in turn were covered with more banana leaves. He left the oven steaming under its cover, took the coconut shells and reduced them to charcoal, which he fired to barbecue some chicken.

Half an hour later we were breaking the hot *taro* to dip into the *palusami* and eating the grilled chicken. Siafolao got little peace as long as I was at his village. Every Sunday he was obliged to cook *palusami* and he never would believe that a *palagi* could have acquired such a taste for it.

Life in American Samoa, despite the rain and humidity, is languid and pleasant. Tutuila is a beautiful island and it is possible to spend Sundays in endless exploration. Most of these require walking, but the tramp to villages such as Afono is rewarding for the views it offers on the way.

If you look closely at the map of Tutuila, you will see only one road to the north-west coast and this leads only to Fagasa. Yet, there are many villages sheltered in the coves and bays on that side of the island. To get to these villages you must do what the Samoans do, either walk or wait for the Government barge that goes round. You can also go to the Manu'a islands on this vessel.

For those on the usual in and out tourist ticket, Tutuila is wonderfully compact for a quick tour. You can go east or west, or if you like first to the one and then to the other. The road west has many points of interest. You go back along the way to the airport and then cut inland past villages and plantations to the great village of Leone, which has the second highest population of any village in American Samoa.

The road winds along the coastline almost to Cape Taupatapu. It runs through villages and then rises above them. A jeep trail will take you from Amanave to Poloa and on your way back you can take an unpaved road along the coast to Vailoatai, a handsome village. When a big surf is running here the huge waves come crashing into the shore, sending up spouts as high as the palm trees. If you watch the waves you will see that they never hit the shore with full impact. First one wing will fold into the lava rock and then the rest of the huge wave will race along the shoreline.

Following the Vailoatai Road, you will emerge again on the paved highway and at Futiga, turn again towards the coast to take a look at Steps Point. You double back to Futiga and turn off again, this time for Vaitogi, where another variation of the ancient South Sea legend of the shark and the turtle is told.

According to this legend a blind woman came long ago to Tutuila from Western Samoa. With her she brought her little granddaughter. A famine occurred and the family they were staying with would not share what food they had. They were dying of starvation, and so the blind woman took her granddaughter to the steep lava rock bluff and holding her tight, leaped into the sea. The little girl turned into a shark and the old woman became a turtle. The proof of this story is that to this day the villagers can call both back by singing a special chant.

It is possible to take an easy way into the mountains. The next village to Futiga is Pavaiai. A road takes you to the village of Mapusagafou and then begins a steep ascent to a high plateau, where at 1,300 feet above the sea nestles the village of Aoloaufou. From here a trail leads down to Aasu, where a landing party from the French exploration party of La Perouse was attacked and eleven men were killed. The French have built a monument to those who lost their lives in the attack.

The trip to the eastern tip of Tutuila is also a pleasant half-day's outing and in some ways the coastline along this stretch is even more beautiful. A Pan American poster features a scene from here with the island of Aunuu in the background. Now, instead of the thatched huts, you will see hurricane houses, and more's the pity.

There is one other outstanding attraction in American Samoa and this is the cable car which leaves from just above the hotel and climbs 1,600 feet to the summit of Mt Alava. The view is superb as the car pulls up above Fagatogo and the hotel. As it rises you can see the disposition of the entire bay, the reefs and the ridges, steep and bushclad. It crosses the bay and rises high above the canneries. Then, almost touching the face of the mountain, it creeps the last few feet to the top. The tramway was built to carry engineers and television transmitters to the top of the hill when it was decided to introduce television education into the school system. Because of the mountainous nature of Tutuila, it was necessary to place the transmission mast in the best possible spot. The cable car runs now for both tourists and for local people who live in Vatia Bay. The best time to go up is on a clear morning or in the evening, when shadows cast dramatic patterns and the light makes the scene even more unreal.

R.L. Stevenson

I saw that island first when it was neither night nor morning. The moon was to the west, setting, but still broad and bright. To the east, and right amidships of the dawn, which was all pink, the daystar sparkled like a diamond. The land breeze blew in our faces, and smelt strong of wild lime and vanilla: other things besides, but these were the most plain; and the chill of it set me sneezing. I should say I had been for years on a low island near the line, living for the most part solitary among natives. Here was a fresh experience: even the tongue would be quite strange to me; and the look of these woods and mountains, and the rare smell of them, renewed my blood.

"The Beach of Falesa".

. . . she had been fishing; all she wore was a chemise, and it was wetted through. She was young and very slender for an island maid, with a long face, a high forehead and a shy, strange, blindish look, between a cat's and a baby's.

"The Beach of Falesa".

. . . she was dressed and scented; her kilt was of fine tapa, looking richer in the folds than any silk; her bust, which was of the colour of dark honey, she wore bare only for some half a dozen necklaces of seeds and flowers; and behind her ears and in her hair she had the scarlet flowers of the hibiscus. She showed the best bearing for a bride conceivable, serious and still. . .

"The Beach of Falesa".

A little cliffy hill cut the valley in two parts, and stood close on the beach; and at high water the sea broke right on the face of it, so that all passage was stopped. Woody mountains hemmed the place all round; the barrier to the east was particularly steep and leafy, the lower parts of it, along the sea, falling in sheer black cliffs streaked with cinnabar; the upper part lumpy with the tops of the great trees. Some of the trees were bright green and some red, and the sand of the beach as black as your shoes. Many birds hovered round the bay, some of them snow-white; and the flying-fox (or vampire) flew there in broad daylight, gnashing its teeth.

"The Beach of Falesa".

To us with our feudal ideas, Samoa has the first appearance of a land of despotism. An elaborate courtliness marks the race alone among Polynesians, terms of ceremony fly thick as oaths on board a ship; commoners my-lord each other when they meet and urchins as they play marbles. And for the real noble, a whole dialect is set apart.

A Footnote to History

Along the whole shore which is everywhere green and level and overlooked by inland mountain tops, the town lies drawn out in strips and clusters. The western horn is Mulinuu, the eastern Matautu; and from one to the other I ask the reader to walk. He will find more of the history of Samoa spread before his eyes in that excursion, than has yet been collected in the blue books or the white books of the world.

"A Footnote to History."

Somerest Maugham

When he came on deck next morning they were close to land. He looked at it with greedy eyes. There was a thin strip of silver beach rising quickly to hills covered to the top with luxuriant vegetation. The coconut trees, thick and green, came nearly to the water's edge, and among them you saw the grass houses of the Samoans; and here and there, gleaming white, a little church. . .

"Rain"

But now they came to the mouth of the harbour and Mrs Macphail joined them. The ship turned sharply and steamed slowly in. It was a great land-locked harbour big enough to hold a fleet of battleships; and all around it rose, high and steep, the green hills. Near the entrance, getting such breeze as blew from the sea, stood the governor's house in a garden. The Stars and Stripes dangled languidly from a flagstaff. They passed two or three trim bungalows and a tennis court, and then they came to the quay with its warehouses . . . there was a growd of eager, noisy, and good-humoured natives come from all parts of the island, some from curiosity, others to barter with the travellers on their way to Sydney; and they brought pineapples and huge bunches of bananas, tapa cloths, necklaces of shells of sharks' teeth, *kava*-bowls, and models of war canoes. . .

"Rain"

But the spot that entranced him was a pool a mile or two away from Apia to which in the evenings he often went to bathe. There was a little river that bubbled over the rocks in a swift stream, and then, after forming the deep pool, ran on, shallow and crystalline, past a ford made by great stones where the natives came sometimes to bathe or to wash their clothes. The coconut trees, with their frivolous elegance, grew thickly on the banks, all clad with trailing plants and they were

126

reflected in the green water. It was just such a scene as you might see in Devonshire among the hills and yet with a difference, for it had a tropical richness, a passion, a scented langour which seemed to melt the heart. The water was fresh, but not cold; and it was delicious after the heat of the day. To bathe there refreshed not only the body but the soul.

"The Pool"

The natives of the islands are devoted to the water. They bathe, somewhere or other, every day, once always and often twice; but they bathe in bands, laughing and joyous, a whole family together; and you often saw a group of girls, dappled by the sun shining through the trees...

"The Pool"

Rupert Brooke

There's only one thing on earth as beautiful [as Fiji]; and that's Samoa by moonlight. That's utterly different, merely Heaven, sheer loveliness. You lie on a mat in a cool Samoan hut, and look on the white sand under the high palms and a gentle sea, and the black line of the reef a mile out, and moonlight over everything, floods and floods of it, not sticky like Honolulu moonlight, not to be eaten with a spoon, but flat and abundant, such that you could slice thin golden-white shavings off it, as off cheese. And then among it all are the loveliest people in the world, moving and dancing like gods and goddesses, very quietly and mysteriously and utterly content. It is sheer beauty, so pure and it's difficult to breathe it in—like living in a Keats world, only it's less syrupy—Endymion without sugar. Completely unconnected with this world

(Letter)

I perfer watching a *siva-siva* to observing Nijinsky. Oh dear, I so wish you'd been with me for some of these native dances. I've got no ear, and can't get the tunes down. They're very simple—just a few bars with a scale of about five notes, repeated over and over again. But its the *rhythm* that gets you. They get extraordinarily rhythmic effects, with everybody beating their hands, or tapping with a stick; and the dancers swaying their bodies and tapping with their feet. None of that damned bounding and pirouetting. Just *stylisierte* pantomime, sometimes slightly indecent. But *most* exciting.

(Letter)

Samoan girls have extraordinarily beautiful bodies. and walk like goddesses. They're a lovely brown colour. without any black Melanesian admixture. Can't you imagine how shattered and fragmentary a heart I'm bearing away to Fiji and Tahiti?

(Letter)

It's all true about the South Seas! I get a little tired of it at moments, because I am just too old for Romance. But there it is; there it wonderfully is; heaven on earth, the ideal life, little work, dancing and singing and eating; naked people of incredible loveliness, perfect manners, and immense kindliness, a divine tropic climate, and intoxicating beauty of scenery. I wandered with an "interpreter"—entirely genial and quite incapable of English—through Samoan villages. The last few days I stopped in one, where a big marriage feast was going on. I lived in a Samoan house (the coolest in the world) with a man and his wife, nine children ranging from a proud beauty of eighteen to a round object of one year, a dog, a cat, a proud hysterical hen, and a gaudy scarlet and green parrot who roved the roof and beams with a wicked eye, choosing a place when to ... twice a day, with humorous precision, on my hat and clothes.

(Letter)

And it's all true about, for instance, cocoanuts. You tramp through a strange, vast, dripping, tropical forest for hours, listening to wierd liquid hootings from birds and demons in the branches above. Then you feel thirsty. So you send your boy up a great perpendicular palm. He runs up with utter ease and grace, cuts off a couple of vast nuts, and comes down and makes holes in them. And they're chock-full of the best drink in the world. Romance! Romance! I walked 15 miles through mud and up and down mountains, and swam three rivers, to get this boat. But if ever you miss me, suddenly, one day, from lecture-room B in King's, or from the Moulin d'Or at lunch, you'll know that I've got sick for the full moon on these little thatched roofs, and the palms against the morning, and the Samoan boys and girls diving thirty feet into a green sea or a deep mountain -pool under a waterfall—and that I've gone back.

(Letter)

ACKNOWLEDGEMENTS

My sincere thanks to the Literary Executor and to William Heinemann Limited and to the Doubleday Publishing Company for their kindness in letting me reproduce the extracts from Somerset Maugham's short stories *Rain* and *The Pool*.

My thanks also to the publishers for permission to reprint the Tahitian chant used in canoe making, which appears on page 9. This chant is from the book *Vikings of the Sunrise* by Peter H. Buck. Copyright, 1938 by J. B. Lippencott Company. Renewal © 1966, by Hawaiian Trust Company.

WESTERN SAMOA

Fagamalo Sato'alepai
Matauti Saleaula
Bay Vaipouli
Sasina Safune Paia Mauga
Fagalele Matavai Letui Lava
Bay Asau Ith Matavai Ologogo Samalae'ulu
Vaotupua Vaisala Asau Matavanu Patamea
A'vata FALEALUPO Auala A'opo Maugaloa Vaiutumaga
C. Mulinu'u Sataua Asau Puna Pu'ap
Tufutafoe Mauga Silisili To'iavea Asaga
Elietoga 6095 3500 Tapu'ele'ele Saipi
Falelima Sali
Crater s Mafane Vaiola
Fagafau 3280 FA'ASALELEAGA Tu
Samataiuta Sapapali Fusi
Fogatuli PALAULI 'Iva
Vaipu'a Vailoa Salelol
Foailuga Sili alelolog
Sala'ilua Lata Tafua Wharf
C. Asuisui Taga Gataivai Satufia Tafua C. Paepaeol
Satufia Apolin
Mana

1 Apolima Fo
2 Falepuna

SAVAI'I

TUTUILA ISLAND

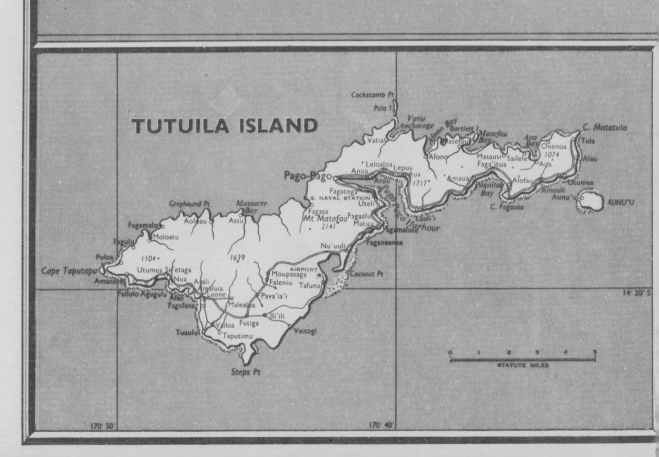

Cockscomb Pt
Pola I.
Vatia C. Matatula
Anchorage Bartlett I. Masefau Tula
Vatia Bay Aoa Onenoa Alao
Afono Masaefou Bay 1074
Greyhound Pt Leloaloa Lepua Masausi Sailele Aoa
Massacre Anua Aua Faga'itua A'ofau
Fagamalo Bay Pago-Pago Amaua Aunu'u AUNU'U
Aoloau Assu Fagatoga Faga'itua Amouli
Moloatu S. NAVAL STATION Bay Utumea
Fagulu Fagasa Uteli C. Fogouso
Poloa 1104 Mt Matafao Fagaalu Sauli'i
Cape Taputapu Utumea Se'etaga 2141 Matuu Fagamalute
Amanave Nua 1639 Nu'uli Faganeanea
Failolo Agugulu Asali AIRPORT Coconut Pt
Afao Amaluia Moupasaga
Fagolele Leone Faleniu Tafuna
Malealoa Pava'ia'i
Ili'ili
Vailoa Futiga
Tuaulu Taputimu Vaitogi

Steps Pt

170° 50' 170° 40' 14° 20' S

0 1 2 3 4 5
STATUTE MILES